THE TOWER OF BABEL

'The Tower of Babel' by Brueghel
(*Vienna Museum*)

STUDIES IN BIBLICAL ARCHAEOLOGY NO. 2

220.93
P249t

THE TOWER
OF BABEL

ANDRÉ PARROT

Curator-in-Chief of the French National Museums,
Professor at the Ecole du Louvre, Paris,
Director of the Mari Archaeological Expedition

48244

SCM PRESS LTD
56 BLOOMSBURY STREET
LONDON

Translated by Edwin Hudson
from the French

LA TOUR DE BABEL
(*Delachaux et Niestlé, Neuchâtel, Second edition 1954*)

First English edition 1955

55~13876

Printed in Great Britain by
The Camelot Press Ltd., London and Southampton

CONTENTS

[5]

LIST OF ILLUSTRATIONS

[7]

FIGURES

THE TOWER OF BABEL

In 1949 I published a book entitled *Ziggurats et Tour de Babel*,[1] which was the fruit of twenty years of research in the soil of Mesopotamia, whither it has been my lot often to return, pick in hand. During that time I had given much thought to how the findings of archaeology compared with the words of the Bible, and I felt that the time had come to pause and take stock once more. I had long been of the opinion that behind the narrative of Chapter ii of Genesis there lay hidden something quite different from what had always been asserted by traditional theology. I had come to the conclusion that the Tower of the Scriptures was not an expression of man's pride. Instead of a clenched fist raised in defiance towards Heaven, I saw it rather as a hand stretched out in supplication, a cry to Heaven for help. This was a bold and unorthodox thesis, but I felt that I could not and must not run away from my growing conviction that it was the right view to take. I defended my interpretation in the course of numerous lectures delivered in Switzerland, in North Africa and in Holland. A large

[1] Published by Albin Michel, Paris, pp. 237, with XVI Plates and 150 figures.

number of those who heard me declared themselves
convinced, and their sympathetic support en-
couraged me to set down in writing what I had
hitherto put forward almost entirely in lectures.
A few years later I used these Alliance Française
lectures as a thesis for a doctorate in theology,
thereby laying myself open to the attacks of the
theologians. Some of them confined themselves to
declaring baldly that my 'theological conclusions
were nevertheless too superficial'.[1] Others did
endeavour to reply to the points I raised, attempting
to reconcile traditional doctrine with the undeniable
facts established by archaeology.[2] In answering
them I sought to arrive at a synthesis, for the truth
is often to be found in a reconciliation of extremes:
in medio stat virtus.

Speaking of my *Discovering Buried Worlds*, and the
first of the Studies, *The Flood and Noah's Ark*, a
Parisian critic, after saying that I was 'terribly
objective, prudent' but 'not a poet' (on this last
point opinions differ[3]), went on to write that I was
calling in question or passing over all the symbolism,
'that is to say the living soul, of religious ritual and

[1] C. Westphal, in *Le Guide*, No. 3, 1950.

[2] E. Jacob, 'Revue des Livres', in *Revue d'Histoire et de Philosophie
religieusus*, 1950, pp. 137-41.

[3] 'These masterly pages are a veritable "Legend of the Ages":
lyrical and *poetical* (cf. the description of the Temple of the Treasure
at Petra), they are imbued throughout with an infectious enthusiasm'
A. Sabatier, in *Réforme*, 10th January 1953.

architecture'.[1] Such a critic cannot know me very well, and I hope that the present study will show that what he says is the opposite of the truth. For it is my chief and constant aim to go beyond the appearances, the tangible forms, and seek out the very soul of these buried peoples.[2] That Tower raised in the middle of the plain of Shinar is the focus of the anxious longing of all humanity to pierce the mystery of its destiny.

[1] R. Kemp, in *Les Nouvelles littéraires*, 8th January 1953.
[2] *Discovering Buried Worlds*, p. 112.

I

LITERARY AND EPIGRAPHICAL EVIDENCE

The story of the Tower of Babel has come down to us in the Old Testament (Gen. 11). It follows immediately upon the table of the peoples who sprang from the seed of Noah (Gen. 10), and precedes that of the descendants of Shem (Gen. 11. 10–25), which leads up to the appearance on the scene of the patriarchs, in the shape of the family of Terah, which was to leave 'Ur of the Chaldees' (Gen. 11.31). Mesopotamia forms the background of all that took place from the beginning up to the period which saw the cataclysm of the Flood. After that disaster there takes place the memorable episode recorded in Genesis in the following terms:

And the whole earth was of one language, and of one speech. And it came to pass, as they journeyed from the east, that they found a plain in the land of Shinar; and they dwelt there. And they said one to another, Go to, let us make brick,

[13]

and burn them throughly. And they had brick for stone, and slime [bitumen, R.V. marg.] had they for mortar. And they said, Go to, let us build us a city and a tower, whose top may reach unto heaven; and let us make us a name, lest we be scattered abroad upon the face of the whole earth. And the LORD came down to see the city and the tower, which the children of men builded. And the LORD said, Behold, the people is one, and they have all one language; and this they begin to do: and now nothing will be restrained from them, which they have imagined to do. Go to, let us go down, and there confound their language, that they may not understand one another's speech. So the LORD scattered them abroad from thence upon the face of all the earth: and they left off to build the city. Therefore is the name of it called Babel; because the LORD did there confound the language of all the earth: and from thence did the LORD scatter them abroad upon the face of all the earth (Gen. 11.1–9).

The tradition here recorded forms part of the Jahvistic cycle. I can find no support for the suggestion of some biblical scholars that it is the result of the amalgamation of two versions. Although that is true of the Flood narrative[1] it is certainly not so

[1] Studies in Biblical Archaeology, No. 1, *The Flood and Noah's Ark*, p. 15ff.

in this case. It follows therefore that the record which we are studying was written down in the course of the ninth to eighth centuries B.C. Its Babylonian origin can scarcely be doubted. It displays too many unmistakable signs of local colour, easily recognizable by anyone who has lived even for a short time in Mesopotamia. The words 'a plain' might well be enough—they conjure up at once that endless flat expanse, now desolate, stretching all around for hundreds of ochre-coloured miles. 'And they had brick for stone, and bitumen had they for mortar': one thinks immediately of those huge Sumerian buildings, constructed of baked brick, like those I excavated in 1932 at Tello, whose courses jointed with bitumen still resisted the workmen's picks. 'A city and a tower': the people (perhaps the Sumerians) who journeyed 'from the east', that is to say from the Iranian plateau, and doubtless from farther east still, came and dwelt in the land of Shinar. Possessing a brilliant civilization, they organized themselves into powerful cities, and in these settled communities, Church and State became one. Above the flat roofs rose the sacred tower, the *ziggurat*, its terraced stories dominating the whole city.

When one takes into account its context and its period, the biblical narrative can refer only to a Mesopotamian population, whose way of life and religious ideas are known to us from the results of archaeological excavation.[1] This is now accepted by almost all biblical scholars, and the story would have presented no difficulty had it stopped at verse 5. At that point Yahweh intervenes, angered by an enterprise that threatens Him in His heaven. His curse falls on the presumptuous building; the people are scattered, and abandon their task. The city which has been the scene of their venture is given the name of *Babel*, for it is there that Yahweh has *confounded* the language of men, and from thence that He has scattered them.

Those who read the text in translation only will be unaware that this explanation presents an insurmountable difficulty. What the narrator is doing is to connect the name of the town, *Babel*, with the divine intervention, explaining it with reference to the *confusion* which Yahweh introduced into the one language then spoken by the whole human race. In other words, he connects *Babel* with the Hebrew root *balal*, which means to confound or to mix. But the fact of the matter is that Babel is quite certainly formed directly from the Akkadian *bab-ilu*

[1] Fr. Chaine, *Le livre de la Genèse*, 1948, p. 166: 'The basis of the story must be the ruins of one of the great staged towers or *ziggurats*, which were used in the worship of the astral deities.' More recently (1951), Fr. de Vaux has put his point of view thus: 'The tradition had become attached to one of the high staged towers which were built in Mesopotamia to symbolize the sacred mountain and to serve as a dwelling-place for the deity' (*La Genèse*, p. 71). I shall come back later to the question of the meaning of these towers.

(gate of the god).[1] I shall have occasion to refer again to this later, when considering the meaning of the tower.

Such is the biblical story, the basic document in our investigation. Let me point out at once that *no further mention whatever* of the episode is made in the Holy Scriptures, and that none of the characters of the Old or the New Testament *ever* makes the least allusion to it. To say the least, this silence is surprising.

At all events it is recognized and admitted by all biblical scholars that the narrative in Genesis 11 had its 'starting-point' in the ruins of one of those huge towers which archaeologists call *ziggurats*, and that the 'Tower of Babel' could only be the *ziggurat* erected at Babylon, in the very heart of the land of Shinar. Since, in the first eleven chapters of Genesis, the biblical record has preserved traditions which are either of Mesopotamian origin, or at least

---

[1] Fr. Chaine, *op. cit.*, p. 165: 'The story ends with an etymology of the name Babel that is in line with several we have already met. There is a play on words between Babel and the Hebrew verb *babal*, which means "he has confounded"'. For his part Fr. de Vaux writes: 'Babel is explained by the root *bll*, "to confound". Babylon, whose name really means "gate of the god", had proudly sought to dominate the world, and had become the "city of confusion", brought low by God's judgement upon it. (Cf. Jer. 51.53; Isa. 14.12 ff.)' *Op. cit.*, p. 71, note f. The Dutch Protestant orientalist Böhl was of the opinion that there had been a play on words (*babalu*) in the original Babylonian story, and that this had been rendered imperfectly in Hebrew, where an identical verb did not exist (*Zeitschrift für die alttestamentliche Wissenschaft*, Giessen, Berlin, 36, pp. 110-13). These quotations will suffice to show the perplexity of the critics.

impregnated with the ideas of Mesopotamian inspiration, it is all the more remarkable to find at this point in Genesis, at a time when the patriarchal family is still dwelling in Ur, a story which must be read (and which can only be properly understood) bearing in mind its historical, geographical and religious context.

* * *

Cuneiform texts. Frequent mention of *ziggurats* is made in Babylonian literature. The oldest epigraphical reference goes back to Gudea, the *patesi* of Lagash (twenty-second century B.C.), in lower Mesopotamia, some fifty miles from Ur. The governor of the Sumerian city refers, among other sacred buildings, to the 'e-Pa, the temple of the seven zones' (=stories), which he erected to the god of the city, Ningursu.

Numerous sovereigns after him commemorate similar foundations, their inscriptions often being worded with a grandiloquence amounting to braggadocio. The founder of the Neo-Babylonian dynasty, Nabopolassar (625–605 B.C.), speaks thus of the tower which he restored in Babylon:

'The lord Marduk commanded me concerning Etemenanki, the staged tower of Babylon, which before my time had become dilapidated and ruinous, that I should make its foundations secure in the bosom of the nether world, and make its summit like the heavens.'

[18]

The monarch continues:

'I caused baked bricks to be made. As it were the rains from
on high which are measureless, or great torrents, I caused
streams of bitumen to be brought by the canal Arahtu. . . . I
took a reed and myself measured the dimensions [to be given
to the tower] . . . following the counsel of the gods Shamash,
Adad and Marduk, I made decisions and kept them in my
heart; I preserved the measurements [of the tower] in my
memory, like a treasure. I deposited [in the foundations] under
the bricks gold, silver and precious stones from the mountains
and from the sea. I caused to be made my own royal likeness,
wearing the *dupshikku*, and placed it in the foundations. For
my lord Marduk I bowed my neck, I took off my robe, the
sign of my royal blood, and on my head I bore bricks and earth.
As for Nebuchadnezzar my firstborn son, the beloved of my
heart, I made him bear the mortar, the offerings of wine and
oil, in company with my subjects.'

It is most interesting to find reappearing in the
cuneiform account several features of the biblical
narrative pointed out above: the baked bricks,
the bitumen, and especially the idea of making the
summit of the tower 'like—that is, as high as—the
heavens'. The people of Gen. 11 used the same raw
materials and had the same ambition.

The work of building called for considerable
resources of materials and above all of labour.
Nebuchadnezzar (604–562 B.C.) did not use only
his own subjects. Those were already the days of
forced labour and the conscription of foreign
workers. This is what he records in this connection:

'All the peoples of many nations I constrained to work on

The Tower of Babel

the building of Etemenanki. . . . The high dwelling of my lord Marduk I established on its summit.'

*   *   *

It is not perhaps generally known that we possess a tablet giving the dimensions of Etemenanki, the *ziggurat* of Babylon. This is the so-called 'Esagil tablet' (AO, 6555),[1] now in the Department of Oriental Antiquities at the Louvre.

The text dates from the Seleucid period. The date is in fact carefully given: 'The twenty-sixth day of the ninth month of the eighty-third year of Seleucus king' (i.e. Seleucus II, 12th December 229 B.C.). The tablet was written at Uruk (Erech of Gen. 10.10), doubtless being a copy of an older original from Borsippa, a town near Babylon.

Since it was first published in 1913 it has been subjected to careful study by expert Assyriologists in an attempt to interpret its cryptic language. Here, as an example, is the description of the tower as it appears in lines 16 to 19:

16: Dimensions of the *kigal* of Etemenanki: so that thou mayest see the length and breadth of it.

17: 60.60.60 (is) the length, 60.60.60 the breadth (reckoned) in *suklum*-cubits. To produce the reckoning of it, 3×3.

[1] This document has given rise to an extensive bibliography, for which see my *Ziggurats et Tour de Babel* (p. 22, note 16), which also contains (pp. 22-8) a detailed commentary on the text. The full text was published by P. Scheil, 'Esagil ou le Temple de Bel Marduk à Babylone', in *Mémoires de l'Académie des Inscriptions et Belles-Lettres*, XXXIX (1913), pp. 293-372.

18: $=9$, $9 \times 2 = 18$. As thou knowest not the value of 18 (here it is): 3 pi (ephahs of seed) with the *sirhitum*-cubit.

19: *Kigal* of Etemenanki: height equal to the length and to the breadth.

There follows a second description, even more complicated than the first, the obscurity of which was for a long time the despair of Assyriologists such as Langdon and Weissbach. Lines 37–42 go on to give particulars concerning the stories, of which we are told that there were seven, although the scribe, hastily or carelessly copying the details, has missed a line out, so that the details of the sixth story are completely lacking.

The detailed measurements, as given in lines 37 to 42 of the tablet, are as follows:

First story. Length: 295 ft.; breadth: 295 ft.; height: 108 ft.
Second story. Length: 256 ft.; breadth: 256 ft.; height: 59 ft.
Third story. Length: 197 ft.; breadth: 197 ft.; height: $19\frac{3}{4}$ft.
Fourth story. Length: $167\frac{1}{2}$ ft.; breadth: $167\frac{1}{2}$ ft.; height: $19\frac{3}{4}$ ft.
Fifth story. Length: 138 ft.; breadth, 138 ft.; height: $19\frac{3}{4}$ ft.
[Sixth story. Length: $108\frac{1}{2}$ ft.; breadth: $108\frac{1}{2}$ ft.; height: $19\frac{3}{4}$ ft.]
Seventh story. Length: 79 ft.; breadth: 79 ft.; height: 49 ft.

Besides these, there were other difficulties which tested the ingenuity of the interpreters, in particular the meaning that should be attributed to the word *shahuru* which crowned the description, so to speak, just as it crowned the edifice itself.

At all events it could be concluded from the

laborious studies made that on a base 295 ft. square, Etemenanki, the Tower of Babel, rose with its seven stories to a height of 295 ft. I have already[1] put forward my view that this building, with its seven stages, supported on its top yet another construction, a temple; and this I take to be the meaning of the *shahuru* of the cuneiform tablet. I shall be returning to this subject when I discuss the meaning of the building. It is not difficult to imagine the impression of power and grandeur that must have been given to travellers and pilgrims as they looked up at this great brick pile, massive, but at the same time perfectly ordered.

* * *

Accounts given by ancient travellers. One of the most illustrious of these was Herodotus of Halicarnassus, who visited Babylon about 460 B.C. In the account of his journey, which contains documentary evidence which has been subjected to somewhat varying appraisal, is to be found the following passage,[2] which incontestably refers to the ziggurat Etemenanki:

'In the midst of the temple [of Zeus-Belos] a solid tower was constructed, one stadium in length and one stadium in width. Upon this tower stood another, and again upon this another, and so on, making eight towers in all, one upon another. All eight towers can be climbed by means of a spiral staircase

---

[1] *Ziggurats et Tour de Babel*, p. 27.   [2] *History*, I, 181-3.

which runs round the outside. About half way up there are seats where those who make the ascent can sit and rest. In the topmost tower there is a great temple, and in the temple is a great bed richly appointed, and beside it a golden table. No idol stands there. No one spends the night there save a woman of that country, designated by the god himself, so I was told by the Chaldeans, who are the priests of that divinity.'

Herodotus also reports that he was told that the god sometimes came to the temple and slept on the bed; and that there was another temple below, containing a large golden statue of Zeus, a table, a seat and a stool, the whole made of gold and weighing eight hundred talents.

Taking into account oriental exaggeration and the prestige that is always attached to objects made of gold (which are often invented if they do not exist, and which are especially liable to exaggeration as regards the details of their number, dimensions and weight),[1] the account given by Herodotus contains precise and valuable information, the authenticity of which has been acknowledged by modern archaeology.[2]

[1] A phenomenon to which every archaeological excavator could bear witness. The tiniest piece of gold picked up on the site usually becomes, in subsequent conversations about the find, a bulky ingot.

[2] The reliability of the information which we owe to this 'historian' has quite recently been demonstrated once again. Speaking (at a session of the *Institut* on 16th January 1953) of the discovery at Chatillon-sur-Seine of a Greek or Etruscan bronze vase of impressive size (5 ft. high), M. Charles Picard recalled that the existence of vases of such dimensions was already known from Herodotus, but that until then none had ever been found.

The same cannot be said of the account which we owe to Diodorus Siculus[1] (first century A.D.), which is ornamented with fanciful details. The precision of its detailed enumerations would deceive no one today. With it, in any case, we have arrived at the stage of embellishment and periphrasis. As in the case of the Flood, the story henceforth suffers endless embroidery, with free rein given to the taste for the marvellous.[2] Harpocration of Alexandria brings back from his journey to Babylon (*c.* A.D. 355) the comments made by an old man, a 'Syrian', on seeing the ruined cities, and in particular at the foot of one of the crumbling towers: 'It had been built by giants who wished to climb up to heaven. For this impious folly some were struck by thunderbolts; others, at God's command, were afterwards unable to recognize each other; all the rest fell headlong into the island of Crete, whither God in His wrath had hurled them.' Was the old 'Syrian' who told of this event echoing the Greek legend of the giants, the sons of Earth who piled Ossa upon Perion, thus directly threatening Olympus? It seems fairly likely; and the incident furnishes one

[1] Diodorus Siculus, II, 9. The text will be found in *Ziggurats et Tour de Babel*, p. 10.

[2] A complete documentation appears in A. Jeremias, *The Old Testament in the Light of the Ancient East*, translated by C. L. Beaumont, Williams and Norgate, London, 1911, Vol. I; *Ziggurats et Tour de Babel*, pp. 33-5.

more example of the similarity of certain traditions among different peoples, traditions that are basically the same, but which vary in their imagery to suit differing mentalities.

II

ARCHAEOLOGICAL EVIDENCE

The archaeological research that has been proceeding now for more than a hundred years in Mesopotamia has furnished us with a wealth of valuable evidence. Since the Tower of Babel was a *ziggurat*, what do we know today of this type of architecture?

On the one hand representations of *ziggurats* are found on a great many monuments, while on the other actual examples have been discovered in the course of archaeological excavation.[1] I was recently engaged in making a list of these, and found it an impressive one. It included thirty-three sacred towers,[2] either actually discovered or positively attested in other ways, in twenty-seven different

[1] Once and for all I refer the reader to *Ziggurats et Tour de Babel*, where (pp. 37-167) the complete documentation will be found. It forms the evidence justifying the argument put forward in abridged form in this study, but is too extensive to be included in a work of this scope.

[2] I include in this figure 'temples on a high terrace', which I consider to be the prototypes of the *ziggurats*, and of which mention will be made later. For a different view of this architectural development see M. Lambert and R. J. Tournay, in *Revue d'assyriologie et d'archéologie orientale*, XLV (1951), p. 38.

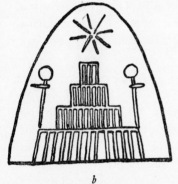

Fig. I. Representations of *ziggurats* found on monuments: (*a*)
Cylinder; (*b*) Seal; (*c*) *Kudurru*.

cities. Comparison of these two figures at once shows
that it was sometimes possible for one city to have
several *ziggurats*. This is an important point. The
total must certainly be greater, for ancient lists
speak of *ziggurats* in cities which have not yet been
excavated, and also in others (Nineveh, for example)

[27]

in which archaeologists have found no traces of them. This fact gives some indication of the extent of the destruction suffered by some of the old capitals, and also of the difficulties encountered even by experienced and vigilant excavators. I may mention here that one more *ziggurat* must now be added to the list: that which I myself discovered at Mari during my last season's digging (October–December 1952).

Before we go into the details of this architectural evidence, let us pause for a moment to look at the monuments on which representations of *ziggurats* are to be found.

*   *   *

Representations of ziggurats. These appear on cylinders,[1] *kudurrus*,[2] amulets, bas-reliefs and on at least one large jar. One also figures, this time in relief, on a bronze table found at Susa.

Carvings (fig. I) are our most valuable source of information, since the examples found come from different periods.[3] One might expect therefore to

[1] These are little stone rollers bearing sunk carving, which took the place of seals or signatures when rolled over the soft clay of tablets. They first appear in Mesopotamia at the end of the fourth millennium B.C. There is certainly a reference to one of them in the story of Judah (Gen. 38. 18).

[2] Stone blocks ornamented with reliefs and inscriptions, deposited in temples as a guarantee of the integrity of certain properties.

[3] The bibliography which I gave in 1949 has now been increased by the addition of detailed studies, of which the following is a

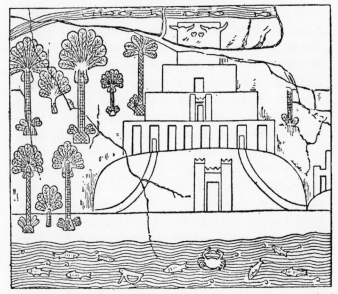

Fig. II. Representation of a *ziggurat* on an Assyrian bas-relief
found at Nineveh (seventh century B.C.).

be able to trace a definite evolution in sacred
architecture. This however does not prove to be the
case. For example, two representations of *ziggurats*,
one from the beginning of the third millennium
B.C., and the other from the Assyrian period (first

selection: E. D. van Buren, 'The Building of a Temple-Tower',
in *RA*, XLVI (1952), pp. 65-74; P. Amiet, 'La ziggurat d'après les
cylindres de l'époque dynastique archaïque', *loc. cit.*, pp. 80-8;
P. Amiet and F. Basmachi, 'Deux représentations de la ziggurat',
in *SUMER*, VIII (1952), pp. 78-81.

millennium B.C.), exhibit only insignificant differences. In both periods towers were constructed in the same manner, with several stories, the volume of each story being less than the one below it, and their façades being ornamented with niches and pilasters. The towers are of three, four or five stories (there was thus no exact uniformity), but although there is literary evidence of seven stories being used, no illustration of such a tower has yet come to light.

It is more difficult to interpret the human figures represented, busying themselves about the foot of the edifice, or even above it (like those on a vase from Susa, seated with their legs dangling). The very reduced scale on which the engraving has been executed (the cylinders are seldom more than an inch to an inch and a half in height) makes identification difficult and always a matter for conjecture. What some see as men busy at the task of construction, others take to be deities and worshippers, the latter preparing a sacrifice in honour of the former.

One of the most remarkable portrayals of the *ziggurat* is to be seen on a bronze tray called the *Sit Shamshi*, discovered at Susa about fifty years ago.[1] An inscription on it shows it to belong to the twelfth century B.C. It gives us a picture of the ceremonial associated with worship in high places. The very name 'sunrise' makes it a monument of Semitic

[1] Now in Room VI of the Department of Oriental Antiquities at the Louvre. A recent photograph appears (Plate III) in *Ziggurats et Tour de Babel*.

Fig. III. Sites of Mesopotamian *ziggurats*.

ritual. It is of unrivalled interest to the student of the history of religion. On the sacred *haram* stand two towers, which, however, show certain features which distinguish them from more specifically Mesopotamian constructions. Built with two or three ledges, they appear to have been used for libations or else for the burning of incense, judging by the cupules which are indicated. Two worshippers kneel face to face, seemingly about to perform ritual ablutions. Close by is to be seen the regular equipment of a place of worship: an offertory table with cupules, loaves of shew-bread (?),[1] pillars,[2] a vase for the reservation of water,[3] sacrificial troughs, a tree,[4] and a stela.[5] All these details are important, in that it is implied that they are the requirements of Semitic worship. The references I have given here are sufficient to indicate the similarities which there appear to be between these rites at Susa and purely Israelite ceremonial. But it must also be pointed out that no parallel to the two towers is so far known in

[1] Cf. I Sam. 21.6; Num. 4.7.

[2] Cf. the references to *hammânîm*, looked upon as pagan emblems: Lev. 26.30; II Chron. 14.4.

[3] One is reminded here of the 'sea of brass' of Solomon's temple, a huge receptacle set up in the court of the sanctuary.

[4] This recalls the practice in the Semitic world of worshipping 'every green tree' (cf. Jer. 3.13; Ezek. 6.13), of which the 'asherah' is probably a reminiscence.

[5] The *massebah*, often referred to in the Bible, and considered an object of idolatry; cf. Deut. 12.3; 16.22, etc.

1. (a) *Ziggurat* of Ur. The triple staircase
(*photograph by the author*)

1. (b) *Ziggurat* of Ur. South face
(*photograph by the author*)

Israel, and that none has been found on any Pal-
estinian site.[1]

The last representation of a *ziggurat* that I shall
mention is that found on two bas-reliefs from the
palace of Assurbanipal at Nineveh (seventh century
B.C.), now preserved in the British Museum and in

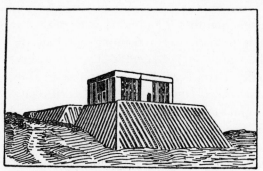

Fig. IV. Uruk: Temple on a high terrace. The
so-called '*Ziggurat* of Anu' (fourth millennium
B.C.)

the Louvre. The relief occupies a single slab, divided
into two as a result of the hazards of excavation.
Represented on it is a four-storied tower, the topmost story being ornamented with horns (fig. II).
This latter detail is of the greatest importance, for
not only does it confer an undeniably religious

[1] It should be noted that the *ziggurat*, a sacred tower, is not to be
confused with the fortified towers (*migdal*), referred to several times
in Judges—at Penuel (8.9-17), Shechem (9.46) and Thebez (9.51).
The importance should be stressed also of the sacred tower discovered
by P. Collart and P. Coupel in the temple at Baalbek.

character upon the monument, but in fact likens it to a giant altar. It is known that altars were actually provided at their four corners with horns,[1] one of the uses of which was to assure complete sanctuary to any who laid hold on them. It is very probable that the *ziggurat* of the Nineveh bas-relief is that of Susa, since we know from an inscription by Assurbanipal that it had horns of burnished bronze.

It is perhaps worth pointing out that the altar of the temple at Jerusalem in Ezekiel's vision[2] must actually have been like a *ziggurat* in shape. He describes it as consisting of three stories on a base, the topmost section being provided with four horns. One wonders if the prophet, then in exile in Mesopotamia, in the region of Nippur,[3] was not influenced in several of his visions by the things he actually saw there: perhaps he had seen the great bulls of the Assyrian palaces, already in ruins, but certainly still visible (cf. 1.5–12); or the huge brick masses of the *ziggurats*, in the shadow of which the exiles tried not to forget the holy city of Zion. There can be no doubt that the sight was painful to them, for in this soaring architecture they must certainly have recognized one of the signs of aggressive paganism. The soil of Mesopotamia was studded with them, each city glorying in its own. Let us turn now to an examination of them.

*   *   *

[1] Ex. 27.2; 30.2; I Kings 1.50.   [2] Ezek. 43.13-17.   [3] Ezek. 1.1.

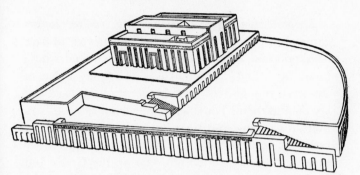

Fig. V. Uqair: Temple on a high terrace. (Beginning of the third millennium B.C.)

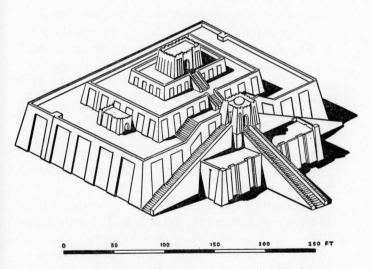

0   50   100   150   200   250 FT

Fig. VI. The *Ziggurat* of Ur at the time of the Third Dynasty (twenty-second–twenty-first centuries B.C.)

The Tower of Babel

Mesopotamian ziggurats. Before the archaeologists came on the scene, travellers had journeyed all over Mesopotamia, attracted by an unknown land whose inhabitants had a different way of life from that of the west, though they were ignorant of the past that lay behind them. Those who came from Europe were more discerning, but their knowledge was made up rather of intuitions than of certainties. The history they had learned rested not only on the Greek and Latin classics, but also, and equally, on the Bible. On the banks of the Euphrates they were reminded of Noah, and even more of Nimrod the hunter (Gen. 10.9), whose mighty deeds were not all beneficent. Indeed, to him was attributed the construction of the 'Tower of Babel',[1] it being said that it was at his instigation that a rebellious people erected the tower, having decided to set themselves up in opposition to God Himself if by chance He should decide to annihilate the human race a second time, in a new Flood. The idea was to build the tower so high that the waters would never be able to submerge it. In this way those who were in time to take refuge there would escape the divine condemnation and punishment.

Benjamin of Tudela (in the twelfth century A.D.), and after him Rauwolf, John Eldred, Pietro della Valle, Niebuhr, the Abbé Joseph de Beauchamp,

[1] Nimrod is explicitly associated with the Tower of Babel on a painted panel preserved in Venice and attributed to Jan Swart (1470–1535).

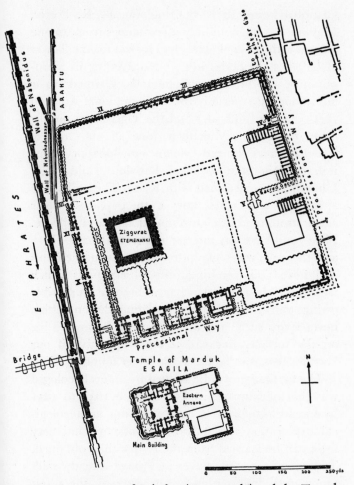

Fig. VII. The *Ziggurat* of Babylon (Etemenanki) and the Temple of Marduk (seventh century B.C.)

Claudius James Rich, Buckingham, R. K. Porter, Mignan—to mention only a few names from among a great army of explorers—had looked for the Tower of Babel of the Scriptures while travelling in Mesopotamia. A number of mounds claimed their attention, but especially the following four: Aqarquf (between the Euphrates and the Tigris, and not far from Baghdad), Mujelibeh (one of the *tells* of Babylon), Birs Nimrud (the ancient Borsippa, a few miles to the south-west of Babylon), and lastly Uhêmir (now identified with Kish). They all made a note of what they saw in these places. Their accounts abound in picturesque details and folklore. If they still have any interest for us, it is because here and there we can pick up from them valuable items of information, resulting from observations which were easy then, but have now become impossible owing to the destruction and dilapidation which never spare such ancient monuments as are visible on the surface. Excavation was imperative if our knowledge was to be based on firmer foundations.

The first *ziggurat* to be studied by an archaeologist was that of Nimrud, excavated from 1845 to 1851 by Layard. Unfortunately, at that time archaeological exploration was only in its infancy, and very little can be learned from the results then obtained. Today, in 1953, we have, as I have already said, much more information at our disposal, the result of a large number of observations made over a period

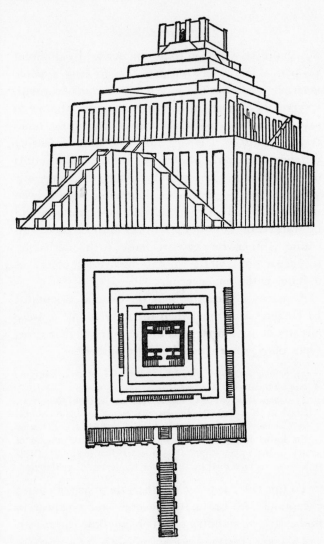

Fig. VIII. Reconstruction of the Tower of Babel (after Busink)

of a hundred years on some thirty sites by different people, a fact which ensures the greatest possible accuracy and objectivity. While one must treat with reserve the reports of the early diggers—that is to say, generally speaking, those published in the nineteenth century—it is certainly true that increasing reliance can nearly always be placed on the results of exploration carried out during the inter-war years. It follows that work done after 1939 is even more reliable. It is right that non-specialists should be warned that out-of-date works must be used with caution, otherwise they are liable to be misled by reconstructions which recent discoveries oblige us to judge with some severity.

A quarter of a century ago, the German orientalist E. Unger,[1] at a time when the data available were already considerable, was of the opinion that three types of *ziggurats* could be distinguished:

(*a*) *Rectangular* type, in the South: Ur, Uruk, Nippur. Access by means of staircases.

(*b*) *Square* type, in the North: Asshur, Kalakh (Nimrud), Khorsabad, Kar-Tukulti-Ninurta. Access by means of ramps.

(*c*) *Combined* type, on a square base (Northern type). Access to the lower stages by means of staircases, and by means of ramps to the upper stages. The most perfect example of this synthesis was furnished by the tower Etemenanki, at Babylon.

To this rule, as to every other, there are of course exceptions. At Eridu, where one would expect to find a *ziggurat* standing on an oblong base (Sumerian

[1] E. Unger, 'Der Turm zu Babel', in *ZATW*, XLV (1927).

type), one finds, on the contrary, a square foundation (Assyrian type). At Kish (al-Uhêmir) the
ground-plan is rectangular and not square.

In spite of these exceptions, Unger's classification
remains a useful basis on which to work; but it is
necessary now to supplement it with a fourth type:

(*d*) The *temple on a high terrace*.

It is in fact my opinion that this architectural
conception is the origin, and in a manner of speaking
the prototype of the primitive *ziggurats*. Unrecog-
nized for a long time, valuable evidence of the
existence of this type of temple has now been provided by the recent excavations at Uruk (1930–9),
Khafajah (1930–7), Obeid (1919–37), Brak (1937–
9), Uqair (1940–1) and, lastly, Eridu (1946–8).

The fact that these sites are very widely dispersed
(Eridu is the southernmost city in Mesopotamia,
while Brak lies far to the north, fig. III) reveals
from the outset an identity of architectural style
which can only rest on a common religion. The
point is of some importance. Perhaps we may
discern an echo of it in the statement in Genesis 11
that the inhabitants of the land of Shinar were *one*
people, having all *one* language. We know now that
that unity was much more real as regards culture
and religion than on the racial and linguistic level,
at least in 'historical' times—that is to say, from
about 3000 B.C.; for by that date Semites and

[41]

Sumerians were already engaged in the struggle for Mesopotamia.

Modern archaeology, then, has shown that in the fourth millennium the people of Mesopotamia were in the habit of raising certain of their temples on a high terrace (fig. IV). The rationalist explanation of this architectural feature supposes that the Mesopotamians were principally concerned to preserve the habitations of their gods (the temple is the *house* of the deity, just as the palace is the king's house) from the ravages of the frequent flooding caused in lower Mesopotamia by the overflowing of the Euphrates and the Tigris. This explanation, however, leaves much of the data entirely out of account. Further, it would appear that this solicitude was felt particularly keenly where a deity was concerned, whereas it was well known that the danger was far greater for mortal men; and yet it is only the dwelling of the god which is thus carefully raised above the level of the plain.

Further, the plan of the temple set up for the deity differs in several particulars from that of an ordinary house, especially in the large number of doors with which it is provided, as if to ensure rapid communication between interior and exterior. The temple, rectangular in shape, consists chiefly of a long central hall, with small chambers giving on to it. From one or other of these rooms access could be gained to the flat roof of the 'house'. A curious fact,

[42]

whose importance was guessed at once, was that in the temple of Anu at Uruk the lowest step of the staircase was 3 ft. 7 ins. above the level of the chamber. What man could negotiate such a step? If not a man, then—since in this case giants are excluded—it can only be that this staircase was that of the god himself. I shall have occasion to return to this point later.

It should be pointed out at once that not *all* Mesopotamian temples were of the type of the 'temple on a high terrace'. There were other divine dwellings, built on the level of the plain like those of men. All that can be said is that in some cities the temple was raised to a distinctly higher level by means of a plinth.

When this base was built in two steps, as was the case at any rate at Uqair, the process of evolution was beginning. From the end of the fourth millennium, through the first half of the third, this raising of the temple became more pronounced, the means adopted being the obvious one of increasing the number of steps in the base. Already at Uqair there were two (fig. V). We have carvings showing masons setting up towers which are to have at least three. The 'temple on a high terrace' has become a *ziggurat*. One of the most famous and certainly the best preserved of these was that set up in the Sumerian capital of Ur. It was rebuilt several times. Particular attention was paid to it by two of the greatest of the kings of the Third Dynasty, Ur-Nammu and Shulgi (twenty-second–twenty-first centuries B.C.).[1] This was some three centuries before the exodus of the Terachites (Gen. 11.31), who must always have remembered the great tower (205 ft. × 140 ft.), its three stories dominating the enclosure and buildings reserved for the lunar god Nannar-Sin. Access to the terraces was gained by three stairways (fig. VI). It is still possible today, as one looks up those long flights of tolerably well-preserved steps, to picture the processions of priests filing up and down them on the ceremonial occasions which required them to officiate in the temple that crowned the third story of the tower.

From the end of the third millennium up to the sixth century B.C., the *ziggurat* of Ur (Plate 1) underwent frequent restoration and modification. Its massive core of sun-dried brick, encased in a solid outer skin of baked bricks set in bitumen,[2] survived all the havoc of wars and tumults. The Neo-Babylonian rulers, who longed to re-establish the glories of the past, asserted the succession to their distant forbears by setting out to build on an even grander scale than they. Nebuchadnezzar, who in 586 B.C. had destroyed Solomon's Temple, embellished that of Sin; and one of his successors,

[1] For the argument on which this chronology is based, see my *Archéologie mésopotamienne*, Vol. II.

[2] 'They had brick for stone, and bitumen had they for mortar' (Gen. 11.3).

Nabonidus (555–538) made further additions to it.
By now the *ziggurat* had grown from three stories to
five and even perhaps to seven: ever bigger, ever
higher. What was being done at Ur had already
been undertaken in the capital itself, at Babylon.

*   *   *

Babylon, whose fame must have filled 'all the
earth', could boast a long history. It is somewhat
disappointing to find that, in spite of all the work
done between 1899 and 1917 by Dr. R. Koldewey's
expedition, so little of its past is known.

Our knowledge goes back no further than the
period of the First Dynasty of Babylon (1894–
1595 B.C.), of which Hammurabi (1792–1750) was
one of the most glorious monarchs. In Sumerian
times the city bore the name of KA-DINGIR-RA, which
the Akkadian tongue transposed into *bab-ili* (more
rarely *Bab-ilani*), which, as I mentioned in Chapter
I, was faithfully reproduced in the Bible in the form
Babel. There can be no doubt of its meaning 'gate
of the god' or 'gate of the gods'. It is, then, at
Babylon that we must expect to find the 'Tower of
Babel'.

The site of the tower was indeed found there, at a
spot now named *es-Sachn*, but the discovery was
disappointing in the extreme. It was not merely
that the *ziggurat* was in ruins. Xerxes had at one

time set about demolishing it (478 B.C.). Alexander the Great, wishing to rebuild it, had ordered the site to be cleared of debris—an Herculean task which was begun but left unfinished. The Arabs had found it an exceptionally useful source of building material, furnishing them for centuries with excellent baked bricks for their own houses.[1] When Koldewey arrived in 1899 the destruction was irreparable. The place was nothing more than a quarry. Nevertheless he did succeed in extracting architectural evidence from it.[2]

The *ziggurat* of Babylon (fig. VII) had been given the name of *E-temen-an-ki* ('house of the foundation of heaven and earth'). It was associated with the temple *E-sag-il*, dedicated to Marduk, the chief god of the city. Standing in a huge enclosure, clearly rectangular in shape (external dimensions 500 yds. ×450 yds.), only its plan was distinguishable. On a square foundation (each face measures slightly more than 298 ft.,[3] it was constructed with a 'kernel' of sun-dried bricks enclosed in a solid shell of baked

[1] The modern town of Hilla, close by, is largely built of bricks from Babylon.

[2] The two basic publications are: R. Koldewey, *Das wiedererstehende Babylon*; F. Wetzel and F. Weissbach, 'Das Hauptheiligtum des Marduk in Babylon, Esagila und Etemenanki', in *Wissenschaftliche Veröffentlichungen der deutschen Orient-Gesellschaft* (Berlin), 59. The reader may also profitably consult E. Unger's monograph *Babylon, Die heilige Stadt nach der Berschreibung der Babylonien*.

[3] It will be remembered that the Esagil Tablet gives 295 ft.—one can hardly quibble over so small a discrepancy.

bricks 49 ft. thick. Access to the upper stories from ground level was made possible by means of three staircases, two set against the south face, and the third centrally placed, at right angles to the façade. Naturally, only the badly damaged remains of these stairways were to be seen, but judging by the height of their steps, it was nevertheless possible to calculate that the lateral flights must have risen to a height of nearly 100 ft., and the central flight to about 130 ft.

These are the only data furnished by archaeology. For the remainder of the reconstruction one must fall back upon the Esagil Tablet and the account given by Herodotus. If we admit the reliability of this literary evidence, we may conclude that the *ziggurat* Etemenanki rose to a height of almost 300 ft. above the courtyard, rearing its imposing mass high above the flat roofs of 'great Babylon'. Although not referred to before the seventh century, it must have been in existence well before that date.[1] Several times destroyed, it was zealously re-erected. It was, above all, the two kings Nabopolassar (625–605) and Nebuchadnezzar II (604–562), who by their embellishments (for example, the covering of the upper temple with blue enamelled bricks) invested it with a splendour which might well have

[1] It will be remembered that the Jahvistic tradition which contains a reminiscence of it was set down in writing in the ninth–eighth centuries B.C., but it is obvious that this rested on a much more ancient oral tradition.

made it the eighth wonder of the world. Today, where once there stood what was perhaps the most gigantic structure of Babylonian civilization, there is an enormous hole, full of water (the Euphrates flows close by, and its waters filter through). The modern traveller, as he contemplates this utter annihilation, as he looks upon palaces that have collapsed like so many houses of cards, cannot but be reminded of those prophetic words: 'Because of the wrath of the LORD it shall not be inhabited, but it shall be wholly desolate' (Jer. 50.13).

On this void we must nevertheless try to reconstruct what existed nearly two thousand years ago. Although Babylon itself is disappointing, in this respect, because the evidence it furnishes is so very scanty, there is no reason why we should not make use of information gleaned from other sites. I have already stated that at Ur the *ziggurat* is still impressive in spite of the erosion of time. The same is true of the two towers at Uruk and Nippur, and it is now known that they were ascended by means of a triple staircase.[1] The methodical excavations carried out at Uruk have also revealed, at the foot of the building and on either side of the central staircase, two small quasi-symmetrical temples. Their disposition is significant, and will be of particular

[1] This information, as far as Nippur is concerned, is the result of excavations carried out in 1950. It is necessary therefore to amend the reconstruction of the tower of that city, given in 1949 in *Ziggurats et Tour de Babel*, p. 153, fig. 97.

2. 'The Tower of Babel' by Brueghel
(*Van Beuningen Collection*)

importance in helping us to understand the theological significance of the *ziggurat*. Near Babylon are two other towers which are still eloquent of the splendours of the past. The first is that at Borsippa (Birs Nimrud), which bore the name of *E-ur-me imin-an-ki* ('house of the seven guides of heaven and earth'), and was sacred to the god Nabu; the second is at Dur-Kurigalzu (Aqarquf), named *E-gi-rin* ('house of the fruits'?). They are the most impressive piles still to be seen in Mesopotamia. The tower of Birs Nimrud still rises to a height of 154 ft., and that of Aqarquf to 187 ft., above the level of the plain. There one can study in the best conditions the bonding of the bricks, which are 'chained' by means of layers of reeds. At Birs Nimrud the staircases have disappeared, but at Aqarquf the position of the triple flight of steps by which the ascent was made is easily distinguishable.

The reader will have noted that so far it has been established that the ascent to the top of the *ziggurat* was made by means of staircases. In one instance, however, at Khorsabad, another method has been noted. In this case there is a ramp which follows all four sides of the building, rising gradually to the level of the court of the temple at the top. It seems that the ramp was characteristic of the Assyrian region, and it is supposed that this method of ascent was adopted for the northern *ziggurats*: Asshur, Kalakh (Nimrud) and Kar-Tukulti-Ninurta.

D [49]

The case of Babylon presented some difficulty: Koldewey had distinguished the foundations of a triple staircase, and it will be remembered that it is generally agreed that while the height of the lateral flights can be calculated at 100 ft., that of the central flight rose to 130 ft. For this reason reconstructions show the former coming up to the level of the first story, and the latter carrying on in a single flight to the level of the second story.[1] Of what happened above that level, archaeology gave no indication. It was therefore thought necessary to fall back upon the information given by Herodotus, who states explicitly: 'A spiral staircase . . . runs round the outside',[2] and to work out a system that would reconcile both the archaeological and the literary data, namely, staircases for stages 1 and 2, and a ramp above that level. Such a system does not however ever clear up all the difficulties, for it is no easy matter to reconcile archaeology, the Esagil Tablet, and Herodotus' account.

Several archaeologists and orientalists have put forward solutions which are alike in that they all tend towards a simplification of the lines, and the elimination of fanciful additions. The majority of these suggestions adopt the idea of ascent by stairs

[1] According to the Esagil Tablet (see above, p. 20) the first story was 108 ft. high, and the second 59 ft., making a total from ground level of 167 ft. I shall be returning later to these reconstructions.

[2] Complete text, p. 15.

and ramp.[1] Divergences are much more marked
when it comes to working out the stories and, especially, to agreeing on their number. I differ in
particular from Dombart and Unger, and, with
Busink, I conceive of a tower of seven stories (fig.
VIII), the last supporting the temple on the summit,
which I believe to be referred to under the name
shahuru in the Esagil Tablet. Such a reconstruction
seems to me to be in accordance with the remark
of Herodotus that there were 'eight towers', and
in the last 'a temple'. Thus, in the purity of its
lines, and not without harmony and balance in its
proportions, the 'Tower of Babel' stood in the heart
of the plain of Shinar. It is understandable that it
impressed all who saw it. Nor is it more astonishing
that it should have had, and still retains, an important place in art.

[1] Among them Martiny, Unger, Dombart and Busink, who may
be considered the most authoritative specialists in this field.

III

THE TOWER OF BABEL IN ART

As was the case with the Flood, the limitations of this study do not permit of an exhaustive treatment of the place occupied in art by the Tower of Babel.[1] So far as I know, the oldest representation (fig. IX*a*) appears on a Salerno ivory (eleventh century A.D.). The oldest in France is in the cloister at Moissac (twelfth century), echoed pictorially, as it were, in the remarkable Saint-Savin cycle (twelfth century).

This long delay before the theme made its appearance is surprising. But from the Middle Ages down to our own day painters, sculptors, workers in mosaic and miniaturists have not been slow to use a subject as inspiring as any, and in the treatment of which free rein could be given to the artist's fancy. It is all the more astonishing, therefore, as François Fosca has pointed out,[2] that we find no reference to it in the work of the 'four greatest "innovators" of painting: Albrecht Dürer, Raphael in the Stanze of the Vatican, Tintoretto and Rembrandt'.

[1] An illustrated documentation of the subject is given in *Ziggurats et Tour de Babel*, pp. 169-93, figs. 109-49, Plates XI-XVI.

[2] In *Gazette de Lausanne*, 8th–9th September 1950 'Peut-on, reconstituer l'apparence de la Tour de Babel?'

We might add Michelangelo, who could have followed up his Deluge and his Drunkenness of Noah in the Sistine Chapel with a brilliant panel devoted to the tower in the plain of Shinar. As François Fosca suggests, this silence may be ex-

a   *b*

Fig. IX. 'The Tower of Babel': (*a*) Salerno ivory; (*b*) Mosaic at Monreale.

plained by the fact that the story of the Tower of Babel was not included among those traditional subjects which the symbolic interpretation of the Scriptures had made familiar to Christian people, so that illustrations of it were comparatively rare.

Those artists who did not neglect the subject often displayed their talent at its best. We should be very much the poorer if Brueghel the Elder (sixteenth century) had also refrained from using it. If I could keep only one picture out of all that have been done on this theme, I should have no hesitation in choosing his. My only difficulty would be whether to choose the Tower in the Vienna Museum (Frontispiece), or the equally powerful one (Plate 2) in the Van Beuningen collection.[1] No one can ever have depicted so well the gigantic nature of the enterprise:[2] an enormous circular mass whose superimposed rings seem destined in truth to reach the heavens.

Earlier illustrators had had more modest ideas. From the thirteenth to the fifteenth centuries, masons industriously trim the courses of an hexagonal tower. The work proceeds peacefully, with no suggestion of fatigue or of menace. Moreover, the number of labourers shown is restricted—three, perhaps, or six; sometimes a few more (fig. IX*b*). With the Renaissance the atmosphere changes: things are seen on a larger scale; erudition suggests that in means and end the enterprise was something out

[1] One of the best critics and historians of art, Dean Jean Alazard, wrote of this masterpiece when it was on view at the Petit Palais in Paris from October 1952 to February 1953: 'It is an expression of Brueghel's genius at its greatest. His scrupulous technique in matters of detail in no way detracts from the power of the general conception. Visitors to this exhibition cannot fail to marvel at this fabulous edifice, which stands amid a countryside of most unconventional composition' (*Les Nouvelles littéraires*, 30th October 1952).

[2] More than seven thousand people are represented on this 30 ins. by 24 ins. canvas. On the same scale as those figures, the tower must have risen to a height of some 300 yards! In accordance with the words of the Bible, it is shown as constructed of brick, the fine mauve tint of which exactly recalls that of the Sumerian terracotta tiles I used to unearth at Tello.

[54]

of the ordinary. Hans Holbein (1497–1543), Etienne Delaune (d. 1583), and Philippe Galle (1537–1612) bend a multitude of workers to the construction of an imposing building. Matthieu Merian, of Basle (1593–1650), shows us a whole city seething with activity (Pl. 3): blocks of stone are issuing from the quarries, thick smoke is belching from the brick-kilns, caravans are arriving from all directions, and, thanks to a circular ramp, are even able to take right up to the summit the materials indispensable to the progress of the work. All this is taking place on the edge of a great city dominated by towers and steeples and cut in two by a river. It is a mixture of east and west: one sees horses and carts alongside camels.

Hereafter this is the dominant note: a hurrying breathless multitude mobilized in ceaseless toil. Moreover, these toilers are under surveillance; new figures appear, no doubt a king with an armed escort. In the Genesis story it was Yahweh who came down to see the tower. Here it is a king, who inspires the work as if a state of extreme emergency had just been declared in the land.

Pieter Brueghel, Rottentrammer and Brueghel,[1] Lucas van Valkenborgh (1530–97),[2] and H. van Cleve,[3] vie with one another in the treatment of a

---

[1] A picture in the Musée des Beaux-Arts at Geneva (mentioned by F. Fosca).

[2] In the Louvre. [3] Rijksmuseum Kröller-Müller, Otterlo.

[55]

subject which is not henceforth to be understood otherwise.

Many old Bibles are illustrated in this way, with only the slightest variation between one composition and another. The engraver Zacharias Dolendo (sixteenth-seventeenth centuries), however, deserves special mention. He portrays not only the construction of the tower, but also the dispersal of the peoples. He shows us humanity being scattered, streaming in long diverging lines away from the cursed building, upon which the divine fire has just fallen.

The way was clear for the Romantics. Gustave Doré rears his tower against a stormy sky. Like slaves men toil to get it finished, with an effort born of despair. Beasts of burden sweat and strain with the weight of the materials that have to be dragged up a spiral ramp to where the top of the tower is lost in the clouds. Clearly some of the workmen are perplexed; others are anxious about the progress of the operations. But the uncertainty and irresolution of those responsible for the enterprise will not stand up against the fierce and impious determination of one of their number. On a huge block of stone he stands erect in an attitude of arrogance, raising towards heaven his two clenched fists. How can we, after that, maintain that the Tower of Babel is not a clenched fist, but an outstretched hand? In spite of Gustave Doré and others who have expressed the same view, this is what I now intend to do.

IV

THE TOWER OF BABEL AND THEOLOGY

The Tower of Babel was a *ziggurat*. Since it is to archaeology that we owe our knowledge of the appearance of these buildings, it is only natural that we should turn to archaeology when we go on to study their significance. It is indeed essential to go behind the outward form, to try to arrive at the theological and religious reasons which must have inspired the construction of these huge piles. Why were they set up?

Etymology does not help much here.[1] The form *ziqquratu* is connected with the verb *zaqaru* meaning 'to be high, raised up'. The word *ziggurat* is used either for the summit of a mountain or for the staged tower.

Early travellers and orientalists put forward materialistic explanations. For Niebuhr, Aqarquf was a platform whither the caliphs of Baghdad

[1] There was no uniform spelling in ancient times, and modern authors write variously *siqurat* (Dhorme), *zikkurrat* (Dombart), *ziqqurrat* (Dombart, Unger), *zikurrat* (Andrae). In choosing *ziggurat* I am conforming to the practice of most British and French archaeologists.

resorted to enjoy the cool air. Fresnel wrote of Birs Nimrud that it was no more than a building so constructed as to permit the priests of Bel to have cool nights free of mosquitoes. The consul De Sarzec, who carried out some digging at Tello, was of a similar opinion. He considered that the probable purpose of these elevated 'Chaldeo–Babylonian' constructions was to afford the inhabitants a refuge from the clouds of insects and the burning winds which afflict those regions for nine months of the year.

Less utilitarian interpretations were, however, also suggested. Victor Place, who excavated the tower at Khorsabad, saw it as an observatory, to which two altars found in the vicinity gave a 'religious aspect'. Georges Perrot, while acknowledging that the staged towers were sacred to certain divinities, nevertheless wrote that people ascended them 'to observe the heavenly bodies'.

These explanations, not without their validity in the last century, can no longer be entertained, now that the documentary evidence has not only been greatly added to, but also subjected to minute examination by specialists in various branches of knowledge—archaeologists, architects, and historians of religion. Several theories are currently put forward, and these I must now briefly summarize.

1. The first connects the *ziggurat* with a *funerary concept*, seeing it as the tomb of a king or a god. The

scholars responsible for this theory were in my opinion quite certainly influenced by a purely superficial resemblance between the *ziggurat* and the

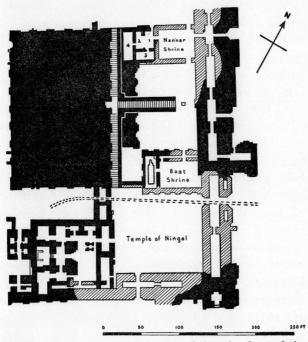

Fig. X. The *Ziggurat* of Ur. Temples at the foot of the tower (sixth century B.C.)

Egyptian pyramid. For while the latter covers and in effect conceals a tomb, the former is merely a graded platform destined to support a temple. Other orientalists have been influenced by certain

[59]

classical and Babylonian texts. Did not Strabo say that the tower at Babylon was the 'tomb of Belos', and did not cuneiform literature often pay respect, in close relationship with the *ziggurat*, to a mysterious *gigunu*, which was taken by many to mean a tomb? I cannot enter here into a detailed philological discussion. Suffice it to say that the meaning of the term *gigunu* is so obscure that this line of inquiry can lead to no positive conclusions.

2. The second interpretation asserts that architecturally the *ziggurat* has a *cosmological* and *symbolical* significance. The tower at Borsippa bore a suggestive name: 'House of the seven guides of heaven and earth', a clear allusion to the seven spheres in which the seven planets moved. To the *ziggurat* at Borsippa were attributed—without, however, archaeological proof—seven stories, each sacred to a planet and painted with the corresponding symbolical colour: black, orange, red, white, blue, yellow, gold, and silver. Without wishing to detract in any way from the effectiveness of this architectural and chromatic harmony, if it existed, it would be necessary first to be sure that it did in fact exist, a point which the publications on the subject by no means establish. The same is true of the colours (white, black, red, and blue) which used to be ascribed to the *ziggurat* of Ur, an attribution denied by several observers.

The symbolical theory is shared in some respects

by Jensen and Father Lagrange, who saw in the *ziggurat* a model of the earth, constituting the private domain of the god, and providing for him, as Father Vincent wrote, not so much a ritual temple as a sort of resting-place.

3. Towards the end of last century Lethaby maintained what was a singularly bold thesis for those days, namely that the *ziggurat* was the *throne* of the god and the true *altar*. Dombart, an architect, adopted this theory, and had no difficulty in finding texts which stated explicitly that the gods loved to dwell on the summits of mountains. Thus the *ziggurat* represented the mountain, whereon enthroned the deity ruled the universe.

4. It is however to the German architect W. Andrae, a pupil of Koldewey and responsible for brilliant archaeological work at Asshur, that we owe, in my opinion, the profoundest interpretation. It is, moreover, the interpretation which agrees best with the archaeological evidence. The *ziggurat* was not only a staged tower. It was a gigantic plinth whose true purpose was to support a sanctuary (*Hochtempel*), the habitation of the god. Further, the god could leave this dwelling, and descend to the lower level of the city—to men. Using the stairways of the tower, the deity could come down to the lower temple (*Tieftempel*) at the base of the tower, and there manifest himself.

5. This theory, although it has often been

criticized, especially in Germany by such experts as Schott and Lenzen, is in my view correct in essentials, though requiring modification in its details. Archaeology has shown that from the fourth millennium onwards the Mesopotamians were careful to provide for their deity a dwelling raised above the level of the houses of ordinary mortals. I cannot believe that this arrangement was made solely with the object of rendering the divine residence safe from the consequences of a flood. The platform, the terrace, were the first results of man's desire to raise himself. But his essential preoccupation tended to turn him even more towards the god whose favour must be sought, and who would certainly be attracted by the offerings laid out on the roof of the house. Rituals of the Seleucid period (fourth century B.C.), which are almost certainly connected with beliefs of immensely greater antiquity, give us details of preparatory measures and ceremonies, the performance of which would assure the success of this operation.

Although these beliefs, and what lay behind the rites (in this case man's desire to bring his god down to earth) may not have undergone much modification, it is certain that an evolution in architecture took place. About the middle of the third millennium men began to construct higher and higher buildings. After the temple on a high terrace (figs. IV and V), we have the tower composed of several steps (fig.

VI), but the idea of the latter is not merely to superimpose one mass upon another. It is essentially a base, whose steps increase in size until they are of gigantic proportions. Then, as the centuries pass, men desire to raise the buildings even higher. Always, at the top, stands the sanctuary.

There is revealed, however, a double tendency in this architectural evolution. It was not possible to conceive of the deity dwelling permanently in a sanctuary which had become very small and which, moreover, had become further and further removed from men. It became imperative to provide at the foot of the tower another temple, of a more fitting size, which would above all be set in the midst of humanity itself. Thus it came about that the complex of sacred buildings included *two* sanctuaries, one at the summit, and the other at the base of the *ziggurat* (fig. XI). The first was now only the threshold over which the deity passed, not without receiving the homage and the offerings of the faithful, as he made contact with the earth; the second became the abode where the heavenly guest might dwell as long as he wished.

But we must look still more closely into the problem. As I have said, etymology does not greatly assist us. Dogmatically speaking, the term *ziggurat* tells us nothing. Can we learn anything in this respect from the names given to the different *ziggurats*? We do know that the names given to the *ziggurats*

differed. Just as, for example, we have churches named after the Trinity, the Nativity, the Redemption, or after a saint, so the *ziggurats* bore names such as 'House of the mountain of the universe' (Asshur), 'House of the seven guides of heaven and earth' (Borsippa), 'House of the king counsellor of equity' (Ur), 'Lofty house of Zababa and Innina whose head is as high as the heavens' (Kish), 'House of the mountain' (Nippur), 'House of the link between heaven and earth' (Larsa), 'House of the foundation of heaven and earth' (Babylon).

The list could be extended, but these examples abundantly suffice. They show diversity, but there is a common basis to be seen in them: everywhere the *ziggurat* is termed a 'house' (i.e. temple), and very frequently the name includes *both* earth and heaven. One case, that of Larsa, explicitly speaks of a 'link'. Thus the *ziggurat* appears to me to be a *bond of union*, whose purpose was to assure communication between earth and heaven. Even when this idea is not actually clearly expressed, it is nevertheless implicitly suggested; for what is the 'mountain' but a giant step-ladder by means of which a man may ascend as near as possible to the sky? Not only in order to touch it, but also, and especially, to approach nearer to the deity whom he seeks, and whose descent towards mankind he wishes at the same time to facilitate.

[64]

3. 'The Tower of Babel' by Matthieu Merian (1593–1650)
Etching

The Tower of Babel and Theology

At this point we must go back to Genesis. Discussion is still going on concerning the historical and theological problems raised by the body of writings forming the first eleven chapters. That these problems are difficult ones is becoming increasingly evident, as much from the Encyclicals or Acts of the Pontifical Biblical Commission,[1] as from the written or verbal arguments put forward by Protestant theologians of varying tendencies and schools.

The general approach in both cases has been to seek in the story of Genesis 11 rather a moral than an historical truth. We also meet once more the view I have referred to elsewhere, that the accounts are 'substantially' accurate, but that they may contain 'inaccuracies of detail'.[2] Nevertheless the biblical narrative strikes me as being profoundly 'historical', abounding as it does in points of detail which rest upon precise evidence, and upon realities to which I have already called attention. But the narrative is even more clearly theological, in the severe judgement it makes of the enterprise undertaken by

[1] These 'Actes', in *Revue biblique*, 1948, pp. 581-4, constitute a reply to two questions which had been put to His Holiness by Cardinal Suhard, Archbishop of Paris.

[2] Fr. de Vaux has spoken bluntly of 'discordances' (*La Genèse*, p. 13), giving an impressive list. Alexandre Westphal had already had the courage to do the same. The reader is referred to his unequivocal remarks on the subject in *Dictionnaire encyclopédique de la Bible*, pp. viii-ix. His conclusion is well worth quoting and meditating upon: 'In Bible study, every victory won by historical truth is a service rendered to religious truth' (*loc. cit.*, p. x).

mankind. By building their city and their tower with a success that is due to their being united (one people, one language), they arouse the jealousy and wrath of God. Their success, which others may copy, is therefore an intolerable threat, which God crushes without hesitation, creating confusion and then scattering them.

This severe condemnation has been taken up again and abundantly commented upon. Many biblical scholars and theologians,[1] some of whom (E. Jacob, for example) are thoroughly conversant with the findings of archaeology and yet do not agree with my conclusions, still go out of their way to justify it, denouncing 'the subtle paganism present even in the most religious of us, which wishes at any price to ascend to heaven and force the deity to come down',[2] or, again asserting that the initiative ought to have come from God for 'man ascends towards God only on His express command, as Moses did on Sinai—and trembles as he goes. Yahweh does not need men to build Him a way of approach before He can come down to earth'.[3] Another writes: 'The Tower of Babel is the very type of the sin which prompts man, not to do without

[1] I should like to stress that this controversy has always been marked by the greatest courtesy. The discussion of our differing views has never damaged the friendliness of our personal relationships. I, for one, am very glad that this is so.

[2] W. Suffert, in *Le Christianisme au XXᵉ siècle*, 2nd March 1950.

[3] E. Jacob, *Revue d'Histoire et de Philosophie religieuses*, 1950, p. 140.

God, but to make a name for himself (that is to say, to reassure himself against destiny) by means of a religious enterprise clearly designed to turn the God of Heaven into a neighbour fixed in an earthly dwelling.'[1]

We must not, however, digress from our purpose. The Tower of Babel must be judged not, as is often the case, in accordance with some doctrinal position, but in the light of the archaeological and historical evidence, and only so. The severity of the Jahvistic narrator is susceptible also of a simple historical explanation: Israel had plenty of cause for complaint against Babel, which it saw as the permanent symbol of paganism and oppression. It is true too—and this I willingly admit—that the pride of man is enormous, and his vanity immeasurable. Monarchs —and not only those of yesterday, but those of today as well—delight in lengthy inscriptions, in making a display of their great deeds and of the works of their hands. All this is abundantly true. So if the dwellers in the plain of Shinar did indeed intend by building their tower to climb up and wage war against heaven, their sin would be proved, and it would be cardinal. But they certainly had no such intention. Are they to be blamed for wishing to approach heaven, to come near, that is, to their gods? That is the problem. If so, then let us be logical: we must also condemn in the same way

[1] J. S. Javet, in *Le Christianisme au XXᵉ siècle*, 29th January 1942.

all man's initiatives such as the towers of Notre-Dame, and the spires of Chartres Cathedral! And then let us admit it, this idea of an angry God who comes and with His own hands sows discord—the source of all wars and of all hate—in the very heart of a *united* and therefore *peaceful* humanity, raises a theological problem the gravity of which we ought seriously to consider.[1]

I have made the point elsewhere, and I repeat it now: the Tower of Babel is the cathedral of antiquity. It is even more than that, for when the cathedrals were built humanity had experienced the Christian revelation, that is to say the perfect message. In the third millennium before Christ the human race was only feeling its way, but already men's hands were clasped in the attitude of prayer, and their eyes had been raised instinctively towards the heavens. In November 1952, near the foot of the archaic *ziggurat* of Mari I discovered a temple full of votive offerings in the form of statuettes of worshippers standing with hands together. Of course they were worshipping and praying to false gods, but the essential step had been taken: they were looking beyond this world. The *ziggurat* which they too had

[1] Moreover, I wonder if it is prudent to base a whole dogmatic structure on a story which is almost certainly what is called in exegesis an 'explanatory' story. 'This "Jahvistic" narrative gives a *different explanation* (my italics) of the diversity of peoples and tongues from that given in Chapter 10', writes Fr. de Vaux (*La Genèse*, p. 70, note *d*). This too deserves some thought.

built was a ladder set up; and that ladder reached towards heaven.

Let us open our Bibles again. At Beth-el, the patriarch Jacob—the grandson of Mesopotamian Abraham—dreamed that he saw a ladder whose top reached to heaven and whose foot rested on the earth. I must quote the text, for in it we shall find what to my mind is the conclusive proof that my interpretation is correct:

'And he lighted upon a certain place, and tarried there all night, because the sun was set; and he took of the stones of that place, and put them for his pillows, and lay down in that place to sleep. And he dreamed, and behold a ladder set up *on the earth*, and the top of it reached *to heaven*: and behold the angels of God *ascending* and *descending* on it. And, behold, the LORD stood *above* it, and said, I am the LORD God of Abraham thy father, and the God of Isaac. . . . And Jacob awaked out of his sleep, and he said, Surely the LORD is in this place; and I knew it not. And he was afraid, and said, How dreadful is this place! this is none other but the house of God, and this is the *gate of heaven*' (Gen. 28.11–13, 16–17).

'Gate of god' (Gen. 11.9), 'gate of heaven' (Gen. 28.17): the two texts cannot be dissociated, and the second helps us to understand the first. The 'Tower of Babel' was a ladder, and the temple it supported was, after all, a 'gate'. It was a strange and moving anticipation of Isaiah's cry: 'Oh that thou wouldest rend the heavens, that thou wouldest come down!' (Isa. 64.1).

We know how, on Christmas night, God did come down.

BIBLIOGRAPHY

A detailed bibliography of monographs and articles dealing with the *ziggurat* and the Tower of Babel will be found in *Ziggurats et Tour de Babel*, pp. 221–5. I give here only a few of the more important works.

W. Andrae, 'Der Babylonische Turm', in *MDOG*, 71 (1932), pp. 1–11.
T. A. Busink, *De Toren van Babel* (1938).
—— *Sumerische en Babylonische Tempelbouw* (1940).
—— *De Babylonische Tempeltoren* (1949).
E. Dhorme, *Les religions de Babylonie et d'Assyrie*, (1949), pp. 178–182.
T. Dombart, *Der Sakralturm. I Teil: Zikkurat* (1920).
—— *Der Babylonische Turm* (1930).
R. Fritz and W. Andrae, *Der Babylonische Turm* (1932).
H. J. Lenzen, *Die Entwicklung der Zikkurat* (1942).
A. Moberg, *Babels Torn* (1918).
E. Unger, *Babylon, Die heilige Stadt* (1931).
The Rev. Fr. H. Vincent, 'De la Tour de Babel au Temple', in *Revue biblique*, 1946, pp. 403–440.

*   *   *

The archaeological evidence is to be found in the various reports published by the respective excavators of the sites where *ziggurats* have been found. I mention here only two volumes, which are fundamental:

F. Wetzel and F. H. Weissbach, *Das Hauptheiligtum des Marduk in Babylon, Esagila und Etemenanki* (1938).

Sir C. L. Woolley, *Ur Excavations* V. *The Ziggurat and its Surroundings* (1939).

INDEX

Index